Original title:
Swimming with the Dolphins

Copyright © 2025 Creative Arts Management OÜ
All rights reserved.

Author: George Mercer
ISBN HARDBACK: 978-1-80587-301-3
ISBN PAPERBACK: 978-1-80587-771-4

Aquatic Duet

In the azure waves they twirl,
Chasing bubbles, giving a whirl.
With squeaks and flips, a joyous song,
In this dance, nothing feels wrong.

Jumps and dives, a playful race,
Each splash brings a smiling face.
Fins like ribbons in the sea,
Who knew friendship could be so free?

A pod of clowns beneath the sun,
Each twist and turn, a giggling run.
Their antics bright in ocean's sprawl,
Chortles echo, a merry call.

So come and join this frolic game,
Where laughter glows, not just a flame.
In salty air, the joy won't cease,
A partnership of sleek, slim peace.

Beneath the Crystal Veil

Gliding under the sapphire hue,
Waddling fish all around in a crew.
With tails a-flip and noses high,
Who knew they could jump so spry?

Bubbles rise like floating dreams,
As they dart in sporadic schemes.
Gigs resonating through the blue,
Oh, what mischief they tend to do!

A latte foam on ocean tide,
These aquatic jesters, full of pride.
With pranks and tickles, a joyous spree,
A watery circus, can't you see?

They swirl and twirl with such delight,
Stealing laughs from day and night.
Underneath this crystal veil,
A life of wonders in each tale.

Glimmers of Playful Souls

With a flip here and a splash there,
They glide through water without a care.
Serenading currents with giggly glee,
The ocean's jester, wild and free.

Twists and turns that shock the eye,
Who knew the sea could make you fly?
With each playful leap that they take,
The ocean shudders with each quake.

They tease the waves, a dance so slick,
Crafting laughter just like magic trick.
The sunbeam glints off their fins of gold,
In this jolly saga, stories unfold.

So come and laugh under the rays,
Join in their silly doings and plays.
Glimmers of joy between every roll,
The ocean's heart beats for every soul.

Liquid Laughter

In the blue beyond, they leap, they glide,
With playful jests they cannot hide.
Tickling the sea floor, they spin and loop,
Creating a film of frothy troupe.

With every splash, there's a raucous cheer,
Giggling echoes for all to hear.
Fins outstretched, they dance in glee,
The ocean's laughter, wild and free.

Under the shimmering sunbeam glow,
They wiggle and squirt, stealing the show.
A slapstick splash, a merry ballet,
In liquid joy, they get to play.

So come join these lively fishy friends,
Where hilarity and fun never ends.
In watery worlds where giggles reside,
The heart of nature, forever wide.

Whirlpools of Wonder

In the realm of blue, they twist and shout,
Flipping and flopping, there's laughter all about.
With silly squeaks and splashy pranks,
They spin like tops in funny ranks.

In jackets of bubbles, they glide and glide,
Wobbling through waters with joy as their guide.
With antics so wild, it's hard to believe,
That nature's jesters never want to leave.

The Orchestra Beneath

Bubbles rise up like notes on a score,
As they play their tunes, you can't help but swore.
With each little dive, they add to the beat,
Making ripples in rhythm, oh what a treat!

They dance in circles, a comical sight,
Some twirl in chaos, others just right.
The ocean's grand band with fins and with flair,
Rehearsing its giggles in salty sea air.

Sylphs of the Sea

In the deep, there's a party, a fin-tastic spree,
With flips and with flutters, they laugh wild and free.
Every wave is a trampoline, each splash a delight,
As these playful spirits dance through the night.

With their jokester faces they poke fun and jest,
Showing off skills, never missing a quest.
Who knew that the ocean could hold such a crew,
Of giggly performers, just waiting for you?

Tidal Tales

Down where the tides spin stories untold,
Our aquatic pals dance, brave, and bold.
They play hide and seek with the currents and foam,
While splashing the legends of their watery home.

In each playful leap, there's a tale to share,
Of bubble-blowing battles and twirls in the air.
With each cheeky grin as the waves roll along,
They sing of adventures in a slapstick song.

Fluid Freedom

In the blue beneath the sun,
Fish dance, everyone having fun.
With flippers flapping, we go fast,
As bubbles pop, our laughter lasts.

A splash here and a giggle there,
A dolphin's grin, beyond compare.
Through bright waves, we twist and twirl,
As the ocean gives a joyful whirl.

Who knew the sea could be so sweet?
A playful flip, oh what a treat!
With friends so finned, we feel alive,
In this watery world, we truly thrive.

Unveiling Ocean Secrets

Beneath the waves, a world awakes,
With playful tales, the ocean makes.
A dolphin speaks in clicks and squeaks,
While playful fish do funny tricks.

Secrets lie in the depths so blue,
With bubbles rising like morning dew.
The turtles laugh, the seahorses cheer,
What wild stories will we hear?

A treasure hunt with a tails' twist,
Every splash is a chance not to miss.
With fins and flippers, we dive and dive,
In this realm, oh, how we thrive!

Heartbeats of the Lagoon

In tranquil waters, we glide and spin,
The dolphins grin, it's a wild win.
With water rippling, joy in our hearts,
Together we burst into silly parts.

A quick dash left, a funny race,
Flip and flop, what a crazy chase!
The lagoon hums with each gleeful splash,
As we intertwine in a playful thrash.

Joyful echoes fill the salty air,
A meeting place for the brave and rare.
With each flicker, more laughter soars,
In this splash zone, who needs the shores?

From Currents to Dreams

In waves we waddle, with playful grace,
Giggling together in this lovely space.
A sideways spin, a cheeky dive,
Bursting with joy, we're so alive!

From currents flowing, we chase the day,
With every flip, we find our way.
A playful nudge, a bubble's rise,
Together we share our oceanic highs.

In dreamlike depths, we whirl and glide,
Bringing laughter where secrets hide.
With every splash, new dreams unfold,
In this splashy tale, we feel bold!

Tides of Joy

Bubbles rise like dancing shoes,
Flipping fins in joyful blues.
Splash a friend, oh what a sight,
Twisting tails, we're feeling bright.

Jumps and dives, we spin around,
Waves of laughter, surf the sound.
Chasing tails in playful glee,
Who knew the sea could be so free?

Tickling waves that tease and twirl,
Under the sun, we spin and whirl.
Coconut dreams on sandy shores,
We plan our antics, always more!

Riding currents, gliding fast,
Making memories that will last.
With each splash, a giggle grows,
Life's a party, the ocean flows.

Whispers in the Waves

Echoes giggle through the blue,
As we dance like we're brand new.
Ticklish tides and silly plays,
Creating laughs in salty spray.

Wobbly fins and goofy grins,
Chasing dreams as the fun begins.
Underwater, it's quite the show,
Who knew the sea was a comedy flow?

Seahorse jokes, oh what a thrill,
Waving hello from the ocean's hill.
With every leap, we lose our breath,
In this splashy place, we dance with depth.

So come join us for a jolly ride,
In this watery world, we take pride.
With playful waves and voices high,
We shimmer like stars in the sunlit sky.

Joyride Through Liquid Light

Beneath the sun, we twirl and sway,
In our own silly, splashing way.
Flippers kick with joyful might,
Gliding through rays of shimmering light.

The ocean's laugh is wild and free,
As fish parade, we bounce with glee.
A dolphin wink, a cheeky cheer,
We gather round, no hint of fear.

Bubble parties and wiggle dances,
Riding the swell, we take our chances.
With playful flips and catchy tunes,
We'll laugh all day under bright blue moons.

Waves of joy, in every swirl,
Here, life's a splash with a twist and twirl.
Drifting dreams on water's page,
Creating giggles at every stage.

Harmony in the Coral Abyss

Beneath the crust of turquoise hue,
Where silliness swims and giggles brew.
Coral castles we explore,
With every splash, we crave for more!

Jellyfish waltz in synchronized fun,
As we tumble and twist, basking in the sun.
A dolphin's laugh, a chorus bright,
Waves of wonder, pure delight.

Under the sea, buoyant and light,
Every flip and flop feels just right.
Silly shadows glide and play,
In this watery world, we'll never stray.

Collecting memories like seashells rare,
Floating together, a joyous affair.
With cheeky grins and hearts awash,
Harmony reigns in a bubbly swash.

Spirit of the Sea

In the splash and giggle of the waves,
Dolphins dance like they're on knaves.
Flip and flop, they tease our boat,
Wearing seaweed like a fancy coat.

Bubbles rise with each wild leap,
These silly fish give us a peep.
They chatter loud, what do they say?
"Join our party, come play and sway!"

With twists and turns, they take a spin,
Who knew marine life could be such a win?
In the water, they make jokes aloud,
Making every swimmer feel so proud!

Under the sun's warming glow,
They're the best pals a swimmer could know.
Costumes of foam, they rule the deep,
With giggles and flips that make hearts leap!

Beneath the Azure Canopy

Below the waves, a grand parade,
Silly seafolk, in light arrayed.
With flips and flops, they swirl around,
Cackling joy like the goofiest sound.

They wear a grin with every splash,
In their world, there's never a clash.
"Catch us if you can!" they giggle in jest,
Try to keep up—oh, what a quest!

Their dolphins sport hats made of shells,
Their laughter bubbles, and oh, it swells!
With each joyous roll by the bay,
They make the ocean a grand buffet!

Through seaweed forests, they'll dart and dive,
An underwater circus, they truly thrive.
No frown allowed in their wet domain,
Just frolicking fun in the salty lane!

Tidepool Secrets

In tidepools shallow, where laughter flows,
Dancing delights in the sea's ebbs and flows.
Silly creatures with bright little eyes,
Making us giggle and wonder, what a surprise!

Anemones swaying like they're in a dance,
While dolphins splash, giving us a chance.
"Jump in, jump in!" they wave with glee,
Join our splash fest beneath the sea!

With each little splash, the tide holds its breath,
As we join the dew of the ocean's depth.
They twirl like twinkling stars in the night,
Underwater ballet, a truly wild sight!

Secrets of laughter and joy so free,
In this realm of wonder, come play with me!
For every wave that breaks and gleams,
Are echoes of laughter and oceanic dreams!

Currents of Connection

Under the sea, a playful crew,
Swirling and twirling, in shades of blue.
With their antics and jests, they invite us near,
"Join our giggle fest, there's nothing to fear!"

They sneak up fast, with a cheeky grin,
"Bet you can't catch us!" the friendly din.
With splashes and squeals, they frolic about,
Teaching us how to have fun without doubt!

In currents swirling, we find our place,
With dolphin pals, we're lost in space.
"Let's wave to the shoreline, then back again!"
Water shimmers bright with laughter's refrain!

So come dear friends, dive into the spree,
In the ocean's arms, wild and free.
For these cheerful guides show us the way,
To embrace all the joy that tides can display!

Dance of the Tides

In the water, they twist and spin,
Bubbles rise, like giggles within.
Flippers flapping, what a sight,
They laugh at waves, in pure delight.

With noses bright, they dive and race,
Playing tag, a slippery chase.
A splash here, and a splash there,
Who knew frolic could fill the air?

They flip and twirl, like stars aligned,
With every twist, a twist in mind.
A waltz beneath the sunny beams,
Their joy is real—it's not just dreams!

Oh, what a troupe, so free and bold,
In waves of shimmer, stories told.
A dance so funny, join the ride,
With these jolly jokers, side by side.

Whispers of the Water

In gentle waves, secrets play,
A chatty splash comes out to sway.
"Hey let's race!" they chirp with glee,
Beneath the sun, it's jubilee!

They swirl and spin, and splash the crowd,
With winks and giggles, oh so loud!
"Catch me if you can!" they tease,
While the sea ticks off its memories.

One jumps up high, a flip in air,
A crowd goes wild—hands raised in prayer!
"I'm flying!" cries, but then it slips,
Into the waves with belly flips!

The sea chuckles, it knows the game,
Each splash and giggle, they stake their claim.
With every ripple, laughter swells,
The whispers of water, oh how it tells!

Serenade of the Sea Creatures

Beneath the waves, a concert blooms,
With bubbly beats, in playful rooms.
Turtles tap their toes to the beat,
While fishes jiggle, oh so neat.

A starfish plays maracas with flair,
And seashells hum, without a care.
Jellyfish sway, lanterns of light,
Leading the dance in the deep of night.

"Hey, let's have fun!" the octopus shouts,
With twinkling eyes, as laughter pouts.
Twirling and swaying, they whirl around,
In a sea of joy, where love is found.

The concert ends with a splashy cheer,
The echoing giggles the world can hear.
In a watery world where squiggles play,
The serenade lasts all day!

Graceful Glides in Azure

With a flip and a flap, they glide with style,
Graceful arcs that make you smile.
Bubbles follow, like little stars,
As they twirl in circles, leaving bizarre.

A dolphin dips, then jumps so high,
Touching clouds in the bright blue sky.
"Oh look, I'm flying!" it chortles and grins,
While friends below start spinning spins.

With a flick of the tail, the mischief starts,
They dash through waves and send out sparks.
Making whirlpools, they cause delight,
Splashing all around, what a sight!

The ocean giggles, a glorious sound,
As they frolic and laugh, joy unbound.
In azure seas, they're the jesters of play,
Bringing smiles to all, come what may.

The Laughter of Fins

In the sea, they dance and twirl,
Flipping joy in a watery whirl.
Splashing water, what a sight,
With squeaky voices, they take flight.

Bubbles rise, a giggling spree,
Nose to nose, so wild and free.
They chase their tails, a playful bunch,
Silly games, always in a hunch.

They wink and nod, a wink this way,
Who can resist? Come join the play!
With tricks they pull and laughs they share,
A jolly bunch without a care.

So if you see them on their quest,
Join their laughter, be their guest!
For in this ocean, jokes abound,
With finned foes, pure joy is found.

A Canvas of Moving Water

In a sea of blue, they paint with glee,
Strokes of laughter, oh can't you see?
A splash of fin, a dash of fun,
Artistry shines beneath the sun.

With each flip, a splashy brush,
Creating laughter in a joyful rush.
They twirl like dancers, light and spry,
Underneath the ocean's sky.

Each dive a stroke, each giggle a note,
Colorful antics as they emote.
With every splash, they bring delight,
An underwater canvas, oh what a sight!

Painting waves with silly cheer,
Masterpieces as they steer.
No need for brushes, just bright grins,
In their world, the laughter begins.

Harmony Amongst the Coral

Coral reefs, a vibrant tune,
Where playful fins dart and swoon.
They bob and weave, a merry chase,
Turning the seabed into a race.

Tickling anemones, giggles abound,
In a coral choir, they gather 'round.
With each flipped tail, a hearty laugh,
Nature's jesters, on the right path.

They harmonize with bubbles so bright,
In the underwater glow, what a sight!
Each ripple sings, a grand ballet,
As they frolic in a joyous display.

With colors bold and tails that flash,
Their laughter echoes, a vibrant splash.
Amongst the coral, pure delight,
In this underwater symphony, life feels right.

Dappled Sunlight and Shadows

In sunlit shallows, they softly play,
Casting shadows in a curious way.
With flukes that glint in bright, warm rays,
They tickle the surface, in playful frays.

A flash of gray, a wink of white,
Chasing beams of shimmering light.
In dappled pools, oh what a sight,
Giggles rising, hearts feel light.

They dive for treasures, shiny and round,
Making mischief as they splish-splash around.
With cheeky grins and a friendly nudge,
Their antics always seem to judge.

Beneath the waves, a secret song,
Where laughter bubbles, you can't go wrong.
Dappled sunlight brings them cheer,
Join their frolic; the fun is here!

Ballet with the Bottlenoses

Twisting through the sea, they prance,
In water's stage, they lead the dance.
A pirouette, a graceful flip,
With swirls of joy, they take a sip.

Gleeful leaps, a slippery show,
With flippers wide, they steal the glow.
Each splash a laugh, a giggle shared,
A watery world where fun is squared.

Fins tap-tapping, a catchy beat,
With bouncing bubbles beneath their feet.
They waltz with rays, spin past the fish,
In this grand ocean, they just swish.

So if you see them, take a glance,
You might just catch a dolphin dance.
In salty foam, they swirl and tease,
A balletic splash, aiming to please.

Splash of Serenity

In tranquil waves, they play around,
With squeaks of joy, the laughs abound.
A playful dive, a bubble burst,
In waters soft, they quench their thirst.

With fins that flutter, they splash away,
Like tiny boats in a sunny bay.
A giggle here, a chortle there,
They dance with sunbeams, so full of flair.

Their flips make ripples, a light ballet,
Painting the ocean in shades of play.
Every leap brings laughter's grace,
In this buoyant, blissful place.

A gentle wave, a tickling sway,
In the heart of the sea, they find their way.
With every giggle, the world feels bright,
A splash of joy, pure delight.

Celestial Sea Companions

In the deep blue, they glide at night,
With twinkling stars, an awe-filled sight.
They wear the cosmos like a gown,
These lively friends, they never frown.

With a flip and a flick, they tumble and tease,
Dodging the waves like a playful breeze.
Oh, how they twirl in moonlight's glow,
A celestial circus, putting on a show.

Each splash ignites a starry cheer,
As comets dance, and dolphins steer.
In lighthearted moments, they sway and dive,
In this watery theater, they're truly alive.

So when you gaze at the vast night sea,
Remember the joy and laughter free.
For in the depths, where they roam and play,
Celestial buddies await the day.

Waves of Laughter

In frothy curls, they burst with glee,
These bubbly pals, as wild as can be.
With spirals and flips, they steal the scene,
Making all ocean life feel serene.

One's doing tricks, a belly flop,
While another's sliding, hop, skip, and bop.
With every splash, a chuckle grows,
In giggling waves, their laughter flows.

They play tag with turtles, spin with the rays,
Turning our ordinary into fun-filled days.
A cacophony of squeaks, a symphony bright,
In the heart of the sea, all feels just right.

Together they whirl, a jubilant spree,
Creating a world of joy and glee.
So come join the fun in this watery land,
Where laughter is currency, and smiles expand.

Merging with the Current

Flippers flapping, all in sync,
Bubbles rise as we all wink.
Lost my snack, a fishy treat,
It swam away, oh what a feat!

Round we go in gleeful play,
Splash a friend, then swim away.
Giggles echo in the blue,
Who knew being wet could feel so new?

Carefree glides, we spin and twirl,
Tail flips whirl and laughter twirls.
Caught a wave and rode it fast,
Oops! A fish just swam right past!

With fins a-flap, we surf the tide,
Moonlit waves, our joy the ride.
In this world, we laugh and glide,
Nature's joy, our hearts open wide.

Vitality of the Depths

Wiggling lines, our bodies sway,
What's that noise? A grand ballet!
Twisting here, then flopping there,
A clumsy dance, with seaweed hair!

Dodging bubbles, make them pop,
Who knew a splash could make me drop?
Oh dear! Did I just trip again?
I think I scared a school of men!

Water's cool, adventures await,
Flippers point, we swim, create!
Giggling friends in a swirling trance,
Chasing each other, yes, what a chance!

Underwater games, a lively race,
Splash and crash, what a silly place!
Elusive fun, we dart and dash,
Oh look, there goes a fishy flash!

The Echoing Clicks

Click and chatter, oh what fun,
Under the waves, we dart and run.
A little flip, a splashy spin,
Who's got the moves? Let's begin!

Echoes ring through watery halls,
Fishy friends join in our calls.
Just missed my turn, oh what a sight,
Plopped down wrong—will I be alright?

With every turn, we play and jest,
The ocean's laughter, it's the best!
Racing currents, we try to win,
Oh snap! I just lost a fin!

Chin smiles wide, we play our tunes,
Under the shimmering light of moons.
A frolic here, oh what a treat,
With playful clicks, we dance to beat!

Spirals in the Surf

Twisting around like a wiggly worm,
In the waves, we spin and squirm.
Laughter bubbles, oh what a mess,
Who knew the ocean could be so blessed?

Giddy spirals, we chase the light,
A silly game, all day and night.
Flippers flail, it's quite a show,
Spectacular moves in an ocean flow!

Surfing up, we leap and dive,
Silly faces, we come alive!
Bouncing off waves, what a blast,
Oh look! I'm winning! (At last!)

Round and round, like dizzy fish,
Jumping high, fulfilling a wish.
What a day, my fins in tow,
Endless joy in the ocean's glow!

The Laughter of the Deep

In the water, we twist and dive,
With playful flips, we come alive.
A splash here, a giggle there,
We dance with joy without a care.

Bubbles rise, tickles abound,
Our silly sounds are quite profound.
With fins that glide and hearts that play,
We laugh at life, come what may.

A dolphin twirls, a cartwheel shows,
As we chase shadows where sunlight flows.
We race to the surface, burst into light,
Each moment's a whimsy, pure delight.

With each wild dive, excitement grows,
A whimsical waltz, as everyone knows.
In the realm where the giggles leap,
We find our joy in the laughter deep.

Echoes of Joyful Freedom

Beneath the waves, we dart and dash,
With wiggly tails, oh what a splash!
A flip here, a giggle there,
Each underwater dance is rare.

In this blue land, our hearts feel light,
We twist and twirl, what a sight!
A school of fish laughs as we zoom,
Our joyous romp dispels all gloom.

We blow some bubbles, what a cheer,
With seaweed crowns, we persevere.
Together we swim, a squad of fun,
Chasing the rays, oh how we run!

Echoes of laughter fill the sea,
In this blissful world, we're wild and free.
With smiles that glimmer like shells so bright,
Our joyful freedom is pure delight.

Beneath the Ocean's Embrace

Oh, beneath the waves, a secret place,
Where giggles play in a bubbly race.
With tails that flip and hearts that soar,
We frolic and play, always wanting more.

The tide plays jokes, it's quite the tease,
As we ride the currents with the greatest ease.
A dance with fishes, beneath the moon,
Echoes of laughter, an endless tune.

We whirl around in a bright, splashy haze,
With every moment, our spirits blaze.
In the ocean's arms, we find our cheer,
Laughter bounces back, always near.

With friendly nudges, we dart and weave,
Creating mischief, oh how we believe!
In this whimsical world, our hearts embrace,
The funny moments in the ocean's grace.

Echoes of the Deep

In the dappled light, we laugh and spin,
With tails that flick, let the fun begin!
We tease the waves, splash water around,
In our underwater joy, we're glory-bound.

Jumping high, we breach with glee,
The ocean's laughter rings loud and free.
There's whimsy in every buoyant dive,
With each splash, we come alive.

As bubbles giggle on the sea's soft floor,
We play peek-a-boo, then ask for more.
Dancing through currents, what a silly spree,
In the echoes of the deep, we just have to be!

From dawn till dusk, we muddle and mix,
With belly flops and playful tricks.
With hearts as light as the drifting foam,
We echo through waters, forever our home.

Ocean's Playmates

In waters blue, they spin and twirl,
With flips and jumps, they give a whirl.
Their laughter bubbles, a joyous sound,
As they chase the waves, round and round.

They wiggle and splash, a playful spree,
Inviting all to join with glee.
With squeaks and chirps, they lead the way,
In this underwater, funny ballet.

Beneath the Surface Dance

Under the waves, where tickles reign,
They twirl around like a silly train.
With fins that flap and tails that swish,
They dance like crazy, oh what a wish!

They peek from reefs, then swiftly hide,
In a game of tag, they take great pride.
With silly grins and playful nibbles,
They send us giggling with their dribbles.

Embrace of the Blue

In the ocean's arms, so wide and vast,
They swim in circles, a merry cast.
With a splash of joy and a twist of flair,
They flirt with seaweed, without a care.

They giggle and glide, like kids at play,
While crabs and fish all clear the way.
With silly prances and acrobatic flips,
They make us laugh with their playful quips.

Echoes of the Deep

Through bubbles and foam, they make their sound,
A chorus of fun as they spin around.
With mischief at heart, they leap and glide,
In this merry dance, they take great pride.

They slide past reefs, so swift and spry,
With giggles echoing like a lullaby.
In the azure depths, they know no bounds,
Creating laughter in their watery rounds.

Secrets in the Tidepools

In the tidepools, secrets hide,
Little crabs wearing shells that slide.
Starfish waving, what a sight!
Making faces, oh so bright!

Tiny fish with goofy grins,
Do they laugh when the tide begins?
Seashells whisper tales of fun,
Underneath the blazing sun!

Octopus tickles with its arms,
Surprised shrieks, they have their charms.
The rocks are bustling, what a scene,
In this underwater laughing machine!

So take a peek, don't be shy,
Join the splash as creatures fly.
Secrets found where waters flow,
In these pools of foamy show!

Swaying with the Sea Breeze

The breeze is dancing, can you see?
Flipping hair, oh so carefree!
My flip-flops giggle on the sand,
As waves come crashing, a soft hand.

Gulls are squawking, what a song,
They join the party, all night long.
A buoy with style, floating by,
Waving flags, oh my, oh my!

Cranky seaweed gives a sway,
Wiggling like it's here to play.
It's a circus, the ocean's flair,
With splashy acts, everywhere!

So let's join in this coastal spree,
With giggles tossed upon the sea.
In breezy lanes, we leap and dive,
Finding joy as we come alive!

A Journey Through the Blue

In a boat of giggles, we will roam,
Sailing on waves that feel like home.
Splashing 'round without a care,
Fish peek up, with goofy stare.

The sun waves back from sky so bright,
Spinning dolphins frolic in delight.
"Catch us if you can!" they tease,
Chasing bubbles in the breeze!

Through coral gardens, colors gleam,
Underwater, a magical dream.
Jellyfish floating, soft as fluff,
Squishy buddies can't get enough!

Adventure awaits in every dip,
With ocean tales on this wild trip.
A splashy wink, a playful cue,
Join this ride, let's bid adieu!

Leap of Joy

With a giggle, I run to the shore,
Watch the waves, I call for more!
Jumping high, like I'm on clouds,
My laughter bursts, so free and loud.

There's a splash zone, what a place,
Diving dolphins set the pace.
They leap and twirl, a joyful sight,
Making waves, a pure delight!

Saltwater hugs, like a wild dance,
In this swirling watery romance.
Every jump is a burst of cheer,
A leap of joy, bringing us near!

So join the fun, don't hesitate,
This ocean's joy we celebrate.
In the splash and play, we find our way,
Leaping through laughter every day!

Kisses of the Cascade

Splashing waves, the fish all stare,
Dolphins giggle, not a care.
With a flip and a dive so grand,
They steal your snack, then play in sand.

A seaweed wig on their sleek head,
Makes them look like they're out of bed!
They wink and swirl, those playful pros,
In a dance where anything goes.

Bubbles rise like tiny balloons,
As they sing silly, off-key tunes.
With every splash, they paint the sea,
In a canvas of glee, wild and free.

Underwater pranks and flips abound,
A joyous riot where joy is found.
Join the fun, no time to fret,
Kisses of Cascade, no regrets!

Coral Dances and Aquatic Serenades

Coral reefs in colors bright,
Dance to tunes of sheer delight.
With a swish and a twirl, they tease,
Fish join in, moving with ease.

An octopus plays a bongo beat,
While clownfish groves tap their feet.
In a conga line, the sea friends prance,
Who knew the deep could throw a dance?

A turtle winks with a cheeky grin,
As dolphins plot their next big win.
'Take the bait!' one whispers low,
But who will bite? They're in the flow!

Giggles echo through the blue,
The ocean's a stage, performing for you.
Coral dances, what a parade,
With tunes so catchy, you won't evade!

Undercurrents of Connection

In the waves, a jester floats,
With bubble hats and silly coats.
Dolphins nudge with a playful nudge,
In this silly sea, they won't budge.

Their jokes are fishy, puns quite absurd,
One'll tell you, 'I'm the best in word!'
But a wave wipes the smile from a stingray,
Who scoffs at jokes, swimming away.

Caught in laughter, their tails entwine,
Making memories, oh so divine.
With each splash, a bond they create,
Two friends found where it's first-rate!

Chasing dreams and jellyfish too,
In aquatic antics, it's never blue.
With undercurrents of pure connection,
In the deep where joy is the direction!

Living the Liquid Dream

Float in the blue, where dreams take flight,
With dolphins laughing, oh what a sight!
They wear those shades like they're on a trip,
With big grins wide on every flip.

Worms on the dance floor, crabs take the lead,
It's a party where no one feels the need.
Pull out your phones, let's capture this scene,
A click of joy, living the dream!

In this underwater bubble of fun,
Every splash feels like a pun.
Join the crew, let your worries dry,
With fins and flippers, we're flying high!

Here's the secret, take it to heart,
Every wave is a new work of art.
Living the liquid dream, what a thrill,
With laughter and joy, we're never still!

Serenity in the Surf

In the waves, we play and tease,
Bubbles burst like giggling bees.
Dancing fins in joyful leaps,
Laughter echoes, the ocean peeps.

Splashing water, what a sight,
Flippers flail, we twist with might.
A fin-fueled cartwheel, I'm a star,
Wondering if I went too far!

Dreaming in the Deep

Underwater, dreams take flight,
Silly seaweed in the twilight.
A turtle joins our playful race,
But knows he's always in last place.

Jellyfish sing, and oh what tunes,
As we waltz beneath the moons.
Flip and flop, a goofy crew,
Who knew the sea could giggle too?

The Call of the Ocean

Waves call out, a playful jest,
Who can swim, who can't, who's best?
We try our luck with silly dives,
Bloopers happen; oh, how we thrive!

Caught a wave, oh, what a whirl,
Through a shoal, I twirl and swirl.
Popcorn sea urchins, tickle me,
Their prickly hugs are quite the spree!

Fluid Bonds

Flipping through, it's quite a scene,
Noses nudge, and pals are keen.
We share a giggle, splash, and spin,
Chasing bubbles like kin within.

Under the sun, we form a line,
Each wiggle, jiggle, feels divine.
In bonded laughter, we stay afloat,
Slick and silly, like a funny boat!

Voices of the Ocean Song

In the waves, they chatter and squeal,
Bubbles popping, oh what a deal!
Flippers flapping, they're quite a sight,
Making mischief from morning to night.

Peeking from below, they play a prank,
Splashing the seagulls, what a big tank!
They twirl in circles, a graceful bait,
"Invisible tag", they laugh and wait.

Fins waving hello, a tail flips high,
Wiggling and giggling, oh me, oh my!
They invite you in for a slippery dance,
With gleeful twirls, you'll take the chance.

Every splash is a story, a laugh, a hoot,
With friends that are sleek, it's one big hoot!
The ocean's a stage for this watery glee,
Join the fun, feel wild and free!

Flashes of Silver

Silver streaks darting, like a live wire,
Zipping through waters, fueled by desire.
With a splash and a smile, they twist and dive,
Bringing laughter alive, making hearts thrive.

In bright blue hues, they leap with zest,
Performing their stunts, they know they're the best!
Winking at you with a playful tease,
Making your heart race like a summer breeze.

Their antics surprise, they're the ocean's jesters,
Completing the tale of sea's playful festers.
With a chirp and a spin, they hop on the waves,
Always cheerful, like little sea knaves.

As they flick and flop with jovial cheer,
Chasing the bubbles that disappear,
Each moment a giggle, a flash, and a play,
In the world of the salty, they sway and sway!

Cascading Joy

Darting through depths, they spin with glee,
Cascading laughter, wild and free.
In a splash parade, they whirl and twirl,
Creating joy with every swirl.

"Catch us if you can!" they slyly chime,
In the warmth of the sun, they play in rhyme,
A frolicsome dance, a wavy embrace,
Life is a game in this joyful space.

With each hop and giggle, they tease the tide,
Like friends at a party, they all abide.
A chorus of splashes, a raucous delight,
They shine and shimmer in the moonlight.

Each flick of a fin tells tales of delight,
As they frolic and laugh through day and night.
A whirlwind of joy that can't be contained,
Within the ocean's heart, endlessly unchained!

Fluid Verses of Freedom

Gliding along, with a wink and a loop,
These giddy sea jesters create quite the troop.
With every dive, they're free as the breeze,
Playing tag with the tide, through giggles and ease.

Twisting and turning, like dancers on air,
They tease the coral and hardly a care.
A ripple of laughter, in liquid delight,
As they frolic and flip in the soft, salty light.

In playful paradises, adventures ignite,
Join their delightful, histo-fish flight.
The ocean's a canvas, their laughter the paint,
A masterpiece blooming, no limits, no restraint.

With every splash, freedom's freshly found,
In the boundless blue, they joyously bound.
In fluid expressions, they jump and they sing,
Each moment an anthem, happiness they bring!

Glimmers of Joy in Motion

In the waves, we twist and twirl,
Playful leaps in a watery whirl.
With a splash and a giggle so bright,
Under the sun, it feels just right.

Bubbles rise, a ticklish delight,
Flippers flapping, oh what a sight!
We race the tides, with silly grins,
In this liquid dance, everyone wins!

Skimming past, like slippery dreams,
Chasing ripples, bursting at the seams.
We frolic free, no worries here,
In our silly world, nothing to fear.

With flicks and flips, we clown around,
In the sunlit waves, joy is found.
Every splash tells a story so bold,
In this ocean playground, laughter unfolds.

A Love Letter to the Sea

Oh, dearest sea, you cradle my heart,
Your waves are a canvas, a work of art.
With every splash, my cares drift away,
Life feels like play on this bright, sunny day.

I write you this note with seaweed ink,
As I float on my back and wink.
Your salty kiss paints smiles on my face,
In your arms, I've found my true place.

You whisper secrets in bubbles of air,
With your swirls and sways, you banish despair.
In this raucous ballet, I twirl and spin,
With you, dear sea, it's where we begin.

So here's to the dance, the splash, and the glee,
Forever enchanted, just you and me.
In the depths of your blue, my spirit is free,
Oh, how I adore your wild jubilee!

Treasures of the Blue Abyss

Dive down deep where the laughter rings,
Among the shells and the playful flings.
Each treasure found, a silly surprise,
Like wearing a conch as a hat—what a guise!

A pearl of wisdom, a wink from a fish,
Finding joy is our one true wish.
Bubbles of giggles rise to the sea,
In this underwater jubilee.

Spin like a cork, twirl with the waves,
In this ocean circus, we are so brave.
Bright colors pop in this laughter spree,
With each joyful splash, we feel so free.

The sea's silly secrets are yet to unfold,
With riddles and games, so rich, so bold.
In this realm of blue, we treasure the fun,
Together forever, just laughing and run.

Luminescent Dreams

Under moonlit waves, the glow we chase,
In this shimmering dance, we find our place.
With flickers of light and laughter loud,
We twirl and spin, oh, we feel so proud!

Each flip and splash ignites the night,
Our dancer's spirit takes joyous flight.
In the glow of the tide, we giggle and play,
Every movement a spark, making night into day.

The stars may twinkle, but we outshine,
With our silly antics, we feel divine.
In this dreamlike shimmer, we're wild and free,
Lost in the magic of our jubilee.

So let's dive deep where the fun never ends,
With fins and flippers, we'll be the best friends.
In luminescent dreams, together we gleam,
Forever entwined in this playful dream.

Dreams Beneath the Waves

In pockets of bubbles, we giggle and glide,
With flippers and fins, we take a silly ride.
A dolphin makes faces, a smirk on its snout,
While we snorkel and tumble, filled with delight out.

We dance through the seaweed, a wiggly waltz,
As fish flip and flop, sending laughter in jolts.
In this watery circus, we frolic and play,
Those dolphins are jokers, in a splashy ballet.

An Aqua Ballet

Under the waves, we twirl in our gear,
The dolphins take charge, and we hold back the cheer.
They leap and they spin, with flips that amaze,
While we float in their shadows, caught up in their gaze.

With each twist and turn, we chuckle aloud,
As they pirouette neatly, and draw quite a crowd.
Their elegance sparkles like pearls in the sun,
In this aqua ballet, we're all having fun!

The Call of the Ocean

The ocean's a phone, and we're calling from sea,
Where dolphins answer with giggles of glee.
They bubble up stories, with clicks and with sounds,
Of mermaids unpinning their tresses in rounds.

A dolphin with shades swims up for a chat,
Says, "Have you seen my cool hat?" What a diplomat!
With a flip and a twist, they swim deep with flair,
Each wave carries laughter, like salt in the air.

Cartoon Clouds Above

Above, fluffy clouds look like puffy sea pies,
While down in the depths, dolphins squish with surprise.
They wiggle their tails, casting silly old spells,
As we grunt like the seals, sharing giggles and yells.

The clouds float like marshmallows, soft, light, and free,
While dolphins make whirlpools, as wild as can be.
In a world filled with wonder, we splash and we glide,
With cartoon clouds above, laughter's our tide.

The Art of Aquatic Play

In the sunlit waves, we frolic and spin,
Splashing about, let the games begin!
With belly flops and silly dives,
We giggle and grin, feeling so alive.

Bubbles rise up like a fizzy toast,
As we twirl underwater, we brag and boast.
Who can out-wobble, who can out-zoom?
A race through the sea, we make our own room.

With fins flapping fast, we zoom in a line,
Each twist and turn, oh, we're feeling fine!
Who knew the sea brought such joyful play?
In our watery world, we laugh all day!

Stunts and splashes, a splashy ballet,
Chasing the jellyfish that flutter away.
We giggle and wiggle, it's a silly spree,
Whirling 'round, living wild and free!

Rippling Reveries

Down in the deep, where the seaweed sways,
We flip and we flop, lost in our ways.
A tail in my face, a giggle-filled kick,
Oops, I'm quite sure that was a close lick!

Darting through bubbles, we race with delight,
A game of tag, oh what a sight!
The sea creatures watch, they join in the show,
With swims and spins, we steal the flow!

Our fins flapping fast, we dance with a throng,
The waves are our stage, a glorious song.
With each playful squeak, we gather and cheer,
Mischief abounds, there's nothing to fear!

Once lost in the fun, we forgot the time,
The ocean's our playground, rhythm and rhyme.
So let's make a splash, raise our voices, take flight,
With rippling reveries that sparkle the night!

Celebrations Under the Surface

Beneath the blue, where the currents twirl,
We gather together, let's give it a whirl!
A party of giggles, a flourish of fins,
With each splashy jig, the fun truly begins.

Throwing seaweed, it's a playful retreat,
We dodge and we dart to the rhythmic beat.
Chasing small fish in a glittering chase,
Every little nudge puts a smile on our face.

The moon beams down with a silvery glow,
We twirl in the tides as the sea creatures flow.
A sardine conga line gives us the cue,
To dance with the waves, just me and you!

With joy in our hearts, we go with the flow,
Echoes of laughter that rise and bestow.
So here's to our shenanigans deep in the sea,
Celebrations unending, just you and me!

Echoing Melodies of the Deep

In watery realms where the tunes intertwine,
We hum little melodies, oh so divine!
With bubbles for beats, we sway in the tide,
Echoing laughter, our joy amplified.

A treble of giggles, a bass of delight,
We compose an ensemble, undersea night.
Riding the rhythm, we break through the haze,
Under bright waves, we're lost in a daze.

Oh what a splashy, symphonic affair,
With fluke flicks and flips, we dance without care.
A chorus of splashes, we sing loud and proud,
In the ocean's embrace, we vanish in crowd.

So join our procession, let the music take hold,
With laughter and joy, stories unfold.
Echoing melodies, a round of pure cheer,
In the depths of the sea, our hearts will revere!

Celestial Choreography Above

In the sea of dreams, they twirl and spin,
Flipping and flopping with mischievous grins.
Their laughter bubbles like fizzy soda,
Making waves while they dance in the moda.

With a splash and a dash, they play peek-a-boo,
Silly antics shining like morning dew.
They leapt through hoops made of shimmering light,
Belly flops echoing, oh what a sight!

Whirling in circles, they join the parade,
Every twist and turn a grand masquerade.
Who knew the ocean harbored such jest?
Underwater giggles, they're simply the best!

Bubbles like balloons float up to the sun,
Each giggle a tale of joy and of fun.
With fins full of flair, they strut their stuff,
In this world of laughter, there's never enough!

Reflections in Aquamarine

In water so bright, they gleam and glide,
Making silly faces, showing off their pride.
With a corkscrew twist and a playful glee,
They honk like seals, isn't that the key?

Gliding past jellyfish, they wink and tease,
Chasing their tails in a fit of ease.
They giggle and splash, oh what a crew,
Swapping fishy secrets, who knew it could brew?

Every flip is a joke, every dive a prank,
Racing each other, giving a flanking spank.
They leap for the light with a splash and a squawk,
Creating a ruckus, their fun never stops!

Reflections in blue, where the jokes never tire,
Dancing like flames, setting the heart afire.
With tails like ribbons and fins like wings,
They spin in circles, oh how the laughter rings!

Rhythm of the Waves

With a flip of their fins, the mischief begins,
Waves bopping along with giggles and spins.
They twirl in the surf like it's a grand ball,
Synchronized silliness, they're having a ball!

Splashing to rhythms from the ocean's deep heart,
Their antics like poetry, a comical art.
With a somersault here and a belly flop sound,
It's a fishy ballet where laughter's renowned.

As bubbles arise, so do giggles and fun,
Every dive down is a race to be won.
A conga line forms in shallow and deep,
While sea turtles watch, half-asleep, half-in-leap.

In this watery dance, the humor's alive,
Each twist of the tail makes the sea creatures thrive.
Under the waves, where the jokes intertwine,
The rhythm of laughter flows like fine wine!

The Jests of the Journey

Popping up here, then down with a splash,
These jolly sea creatures sure know how to dash.
With chirpy little chats and giggles galore,
They play tag with currents, who could ask for more?

Skipping along like they're late for a date,
Transforming the ocean into a grand buffet plate.
They trade silly jokes like fish in a stream,
Floating on laughter, it's the ultimate dream!

With a wink and a nudge, they plot and they scheme,
Making splashy comedies like bubbles that gleam.
They leap through the tides, oh what a delight!
This jesting adventure is purely outta sight!

Tales of the sea echo back to the shore,
Whispering secrets, inviting for more.
As sunbeams dance down on the ocean's grand stage,
These playful companions are filled with pure gage!

Fluid Connections

In a splashy dance beneath the sun,
Flippers flail, and hearts are won.
With squeaky sounds and slippery play,
We twirl and spin, come what may.

A dolphin tricks with a playful grin,
I mimic back, let the laughter spin.
With slippery friends, we make a team,
Chasing bubbles, chasing dreams.

A flip, a twist, in a watery show,
Rolling in circles, to and fro.
Their chuckles echo, oh what a treat,
In this world of wet, life feels so sweet.

As we glide through waves and froth,
Balanced on water, we saunter forth.
With giggles loud and splashes bright,
Dancing in fun, it feels so right.

The Chorus Under the Waves

In the deep where the bubbles bloom,
Silly swimsuits make me assume.
A choir of clicks and tippy-toe twirls,
Underwater giggles make my heart whirl.

With a leap and a skip, oh what a scene,
Dolphins dive deep, swift and keen.
I try to keep up, but they zoom right past,
Like cheeky jesters having a blast.

Their fins like sails, catching the fun,
In this ocean dance, we're all number one.
Flinging water and dodging the spray,
A chorus of laughter, we play all day.

Chasing fish who dart and dive,
With slippery pals, we come alive.
As bubbles rise in a jolly tune,
Our laughter fills, a watery boon.

Navigating the Liquid World

In this vast blue, we bounce and sway,
With fins flapping in a kooky ballet.
Beneath the waves, we twist and glide,
In this liquid realm, we take a ride.

With flicks of tails, we spin and tumble,
Laughter erupts in a playful jumble.
I'm the clown fish, wearing a grin,
While dolphins flip, I try to win.

Navigating currents, we weave and swirl,
In this bubbly kingdom, antics unfurl.
They tease and play as I try to chase,
With every splash, I'm losing grace.

In the depths of blue, joy freely flows,
Disguised as fish, we'll put on a show.
With watery winks and silly glee,
In this joyful dance, we're forever free.

Embracing the Blue Horizon

In a sea of giggles, we take a dive,
Splashing about, feeling so alive!
Flipping and flopping with silly glee,
Fins all a-flutter, just you and me.

A pod of mischief, we race and twirl,
Making a whirlpool, oh what a swirl!
With bubbles of laughter, we float through the day,
Why should humans have all the fun anyway?

We trade in our goggles for curious eyes,
Pretending to be fish in a grand disguise.
A wiggle, a wiggle, a twist in the tide,
Who knew that joy could be found in the wide?

As the sun dips low, we giggle and play,
Planning our pranks for another bright day.
With water so clear and spirits so bright,
We'll swim through the laughter, till the last light.

Tales from Coral Kingdoms

Beneath the waves where the colors explode,
We crack coral jokes on our underwater road.
A starfish with puns is our favorite friend,
Telling tall tales that never quite end.

A turtle named Ted lost his hat to a wave,
He shrieked like a whale, oh how he misbehaved!
With fins full of mirth, we giggle and chime,
Making a scene, oh, isn't it prime?

We wriggle and jive as the seaweed sways,
Playing tag with a crab, we dance in the rays.
With every flip, laughter circles around,
In the coral kingdoms, joy knows no bound.

As bubbles rise high, we chase after dreams,
In our silly realm, everything gleams.
So come join the frolic in waters so wild,
Coral kingdoms await; let your heart be a child!

Navigating the Abyss

In the deep where the dark holds secrets untold,
Here comes the crew, being daring and bold.
With winks and strange flops, we zigzag and dash,
Dancing with shadows in a splashy bash.

A squid with a mustache joins the hoot and the holler,
Every tentacle waving, getting funnier, a caller.
We challenge the currents to pick up the pace,
As laughter echoes in this odd aquatic space.

Toothed fish in glasses swim right past the herd,
"Drop those old fables!" is the sentence absurd.
Each swirl brings a chuckle, a whimsical tease,
In this underwater circus, we do just as we please.

This deep dark abyss is a playground you see,
With silly surprises and ticklish glee!
As we bubble and bounce, confounding the night,
We dance with the sea and bathe in the light.

Beneath the Sunlit Surface

Beneath the rays where the sea sparkles bright,
We giggle and splash from morning till night.
With silly sea creatures all wriggling near,
Our laughter is music, as we'd disappear.

A dolphin with socks swirls in for a joke,
His flippers a-twirl, he smirks as he spoke.
"Why did the fish swim in a straight line?"
"Because curves make it hard to sip on some brine!"

We practice our twirls, we leap with great flair,
While sea turtles cheer like they just don't care.
The seahorses groan, "We can't keep this up!"
While fishies around break into a "what's up?"

With sunlight above and the waves all aglow,
We create our own magic with each splashing show.
So bring your own quirk, your fun-loving spree—
Beneath the sunlit surface, there's joy in the sea!

Crystal Caverns Beneath

In crystal caves where bubbles play,
Silly fish dance, making my day.
I tried to join, but tripped on a shell,
Now I'm rolling, oh well, oh well!

Bright colors swirl, a comedic sight,
A seahorse giggles, what a delight!
They wink and flaunt their tiny flair,
While I just float—oh, the salty air!

A clam begins to hum a tune,
I clap my fins, thinking I'm a boon.
But a rubber ducky floats on by,
And I burst out laughing, oh my, oh my!

With jellyfish jiggling all around,
I slip and slide with a silly bound.
In caverns cool, we play and tease,
Who knew the ocean was such a breeze!

Lost in the Blue Reverie

In deep blue waters, my head went low,
I saw a fish in a funky bow.
It teased me plenty, what a cutie,
While sea cucumbers danced, oh so fruity!

A crab with glasses scuttled near,
Said, "Join the conga, have no fear!"
I stumbled once, then twice, then thrice,
While barnacles giggled—oh, so nice!

A dolphin flips, displaying flair,
Spinning like a gymnast, without a care.
I tried to copy with flair and glee,
But tangled in seaweed; oh, woe is me!

As laughter echoes through the sea's embrace,
I flail and splash in this undersea race.
With friends like these, I can't feel blue,
Who needs a map when you've got this crew?

Dreams of the Sea and Sky

In the dreamy waves where silliness reigns,
A dolphin drags me, but I have no chains.
We chase the bubbles, laughing so loud,
While a starfish grins, feeling so proud.

With a flip and a splash, we dance in the spray,
Bubble-clowns spin and whirl, hey, hooray!
A turtle in shades, oh what a sight,
Says, "Life's a beach, let's party tonight!"

We surf on the waves, our laughter a song,
To the rhythm of water, we all belong.
As gulls circle overhead, we twist and twirl,
And make silly faces, giving them a whirl!

In dreams of the sea, in frolic and fun,
The ocean's a playground—we're never done.
With each silly splash, a joy we find,
In depths of the sea, true friends intertwined!

A Touch of Saltwater Magic

With swirls of spray and giggles galore,
I squeezed right past a clam's open door.
He yelled, "Hey buddy, where's the fire?"
But I was too busy, my joy climbing higher!

A dolphin in shades, oh so chic,
Said, "Wanna race?" I squeaked, "Let's sneak!"
We zoom through the water, swift as can be,
But my flip went wrong, and I bumped a sea tree!

The jellyfish jive, glowing bright in the night,
Inviting us all to join in their flight.
But I tangled my fins, oh what a sight,
Flopping and flailing, try as I might!

As we frolic and splash, the magic is clear,
In this world of laughter, who needs to steer?
With antics so wild and friends by my side,
A touch of saltwater, where joy cannot hide!

Harmony in Liquid Light

In liquid paths where bubbles dance,
Fishy friends glide with a prance.
Twirling tails, a splashy sight,
Giggling in the warm sunlight.

Giggles echo, fins take flight,
Who knew fish could be so bright?
They wink and whirl with joyful glee,
Even wore a hat, oh so fancy!

Bubbles rise in playful cheer,
With a wink, they disappear.
Echoes of laughter fill the sea,
A choir of whimsy wild and free.

In this world of aqua dreams,
Life's an endless game, or so it seems.
Join the party; it's a delight,
In harmony, we splash all night.

Playful Flukes and Flippers

Beneath the waves, a curious crew,
Flippers flapping, just for you.
They dance and dive with such great style,
Every leap brings out a smile.

One fin flips a fishy friend,
Oh, what a sight! Will it ever end?
With giggles echoing through the blue,
A wiggling dance, oh what a view!

Swirls and twirls, a splashy thrill,
Chasing each other without a chill.
One tries to somersault, oh dear!
Lands on a float, can you hear?

With playful splashes all around,
In silly antics, joy is found.
What a frolic, a fun parade,
In the grand sea, no charade!

Chasing Ripples

Ripples shimmer, laughter rings,
Curly tails on magical flings.
A little race beneath the waves,
Each twist and turn, a thrill that saves.

"Catch me if you can!" calls a cheeky fish,
While munching on a bubble-gum swish.
With flukes held high, they wiggle and sway,
Come join the fun, don't delay!

Swirling currents, oh what a chase,
They slide and glide, a watery race.
Every twist brings giggles anew,
Even the seashells cheer, who knew?

Bubbles form a giggling whirl,
In this ocean, laughter will unfurl.
With each ripple, joy forever stays,
In this world of fun-filled plays.

The Silhouettes of Freedom

In shadows cast where dolphins roam,
They frolic freely, far from home.
With a leap and swish, they tease the tide,
A splash, a giggle, oh how they glide!

Gliding between the surf and foam,
With flurries of joy, they make their dome.
Each playful nudge a game of tag,
Holding on tight, and never lag!

Lunchtime tricks with a twist of sprout,
Who knew kelp could be this stout?
They munch and crunch, a delicious feast,
In revelry, the laughter's increased!

Through echoes and tides, they know no bounds,
In every wave, a symphony sounds.
So come and join the swimming spree,
In silhouettes of joy, wild and free!

The Language of Splash

In water's embrace, we dive with glee,
Flippered friends join our wild spree.
They chatter in clicks, a bubbly tune,
While we bob along, under the moon.

A gentle nudge from a whiskered mate,
Plays tricks with tides, we navigate.
With spins and twirls, the laughter flows,
As we slick through waves like slippery prose.

Count the fish in a swirling dance,
Every flip a chance for a playful prance.
They wear their smiles in scales and fins,
While we crack jokes about our underwater spins.

The sea's our stage, with bubbles galore,
We audition each splash, always wanting more.
The ocean's laughter, a perfect partner,
With dolphins playing, we're never a loner.

Celestial Ribbon of Waves

Oh, the sky above, a canvas wide,
We launch ourselves on a tidal ride.
Bubbles rise, our giggles burst,
As we twist and twirl, quenching our thirst.

Stars glimmer down in the briny pool,
As we leap like fools, no rules, just cool.
Flippers flutter, a merry ballet,
While marine pals tease in their playful way.

With splashes like paint, every hue,
Creating a masterpiece, just me and you.
The waves tell secrets in a salty brew,
As laughter dances under skies of blue.

As nightfall serenades our playful spree,
We're the clowns of the ocean, wild and free.
With a wink and a flip, a splish and a flash,
We ride the night tide, a celestial splash!

Emotions in the Estuary

In shallows where the giggles bloom,
We frolic and somersault, dispelling gloom.
Beneath the sun, our worries cease,
Here, every splash is a moment of peace.

The briny breeze carries tales of cheer,
With every wave, mischief's near.
A dolphin grins, I swear it's true,
As we steal their spotlight, just me and you.

Where the rivers meet with a salty kiss,
We drift in joy, lost in bliss.
Jellyfish dance, their antics amaze,
While we invent games, in a watery haze.

A chorus of laughter, our symphony sings,
In estuarine depths, joy truly springs.
With fins and flops, our hearts intertwine,
As we ride the waters, on a whim divine.

Playwrights of the Aquatic Stage

With bubbles as props, we craft our play,
Fin-tastic dramas, in our own quirky way.
A flip here, a splash there, the plot thickens quick,
As we improvise scenes, timing's the trick.

The dolphins direct, with wiggles and swirls,
While we take center stage, giving it twirls.
A pinch of chaos, a swirl of delight,
As we jest and we jive, from day into night.

The sea is our theater, waves our applause,
Each leap a standing ovation, no time to pause.
With laughter as lines and splashes as cues,
We captivate tides with our unbeatable views.

As curtain calls come, we bask in our glow,
Our roles are eternal, as we're in the flow.
With fins as our agents, we'll always be sage,
The whimsical creators of this aquatic stage.

www.ingramcontent.com/pod-product-compliance
Lightning Source LLC
Chambersburg PA
CBHW051732290426
43661CB00122B/238